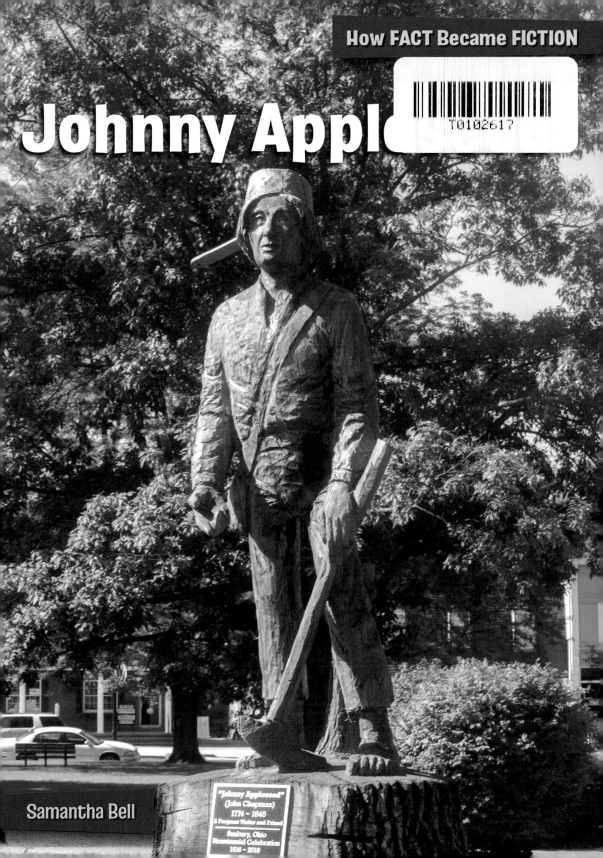

How FACT Became FICTION

Johnny Apple

Samantha Bell

"Johnny Appleseed"
(John Chapman)
1774 ~ 1845
A Frequent Visitor and Friend

Sunbury, Ohio
Bicentennial Celebration
1816 ~ 2016

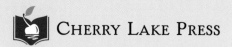
CHERRY LAKE PRESS

Published in the United States of America by Cherry Lake Publishing Group
Ann Arbor, Michigan
www.cherrylakepublishing.com

Reading Adviser: Beth Walker Gambro, MS, Ed., Reading Consultant, Yorkville, IL
Content Adviser: Heather Bruegl, M.A. (Oneida/Stockbridge-Munsee) Historian-Indigenous Consultant-Lecturer

Photo Credits: © Mark Calvert/Dreamstime.com, cover, title page; H. S. Knapp, Public domain, via Wikimedia
Commons, 5; © Ground Picture/Shutterstock, 6; © agrofruti/Shutterstock, 7; © goszczal/Shutterstock, 8; © Larry
Metayer/Dreamstime.com, 9; Rochelle Karp, CC BY-SA 3.0 via Wikimedia Commons, 10; Photograph in the Carol M.
Highsmith Archive, Library of Congress, Prints and Photographs Division, 11; Unknown author, Public domain, via
Wikimedia Commons, 13; Roseohioresident, Public domain, via Wikimedia Commons, 14; John Cary, Public domain,
via Wikimedia Commons, 15; © Photosbypatrik/Shutterstock, 17; Benjamin Fiske Barrett, Public domain, via Wikimedia
Commons, 18; © Olga_i/Shutterstock, 19; Unknown author, Public domain, via Wikimedia Commons, 21; Unknown
photographer, Public domain, via Wikimedia Commons, 22; Unknown author, Public domain, via Wikimedia Commons, 24;
© Triple_D Studio/Shutterstock, 25; Per Krafft the Elder, Public domain, via Wikimedia Commons, 27; © Reshetnikov_art/
Shutterstock, 29

Cherry Lake Press is an imprint of Cherry Lake Publishing Group.

Library of Congress Cataloging-in-Publication Data has been filed and is available at catalog.loc.gov.

Cherry Lake Publishing Group would like to acknowledge the work of the Partnership for 21st Century Learning,
a Network of Battelle for Kids. Please visit http://www.battelleforkids.org/networks/p21 for more information.

Printed in the United States of America
Corporate Graphics

Note from publisher: Websites change regularly, and their future contents are outside of our control.
Supervise children when conducting any recommended online searches for extended learning opportunities.

Samantha Bell was born and raised near Orlando, Florida. She grew up in a family of
eight kids and all kinds of pets, including goats, chickens, cats, dogs, rabbits, horses,
parakeets, hamsters, guinea pigs, a monkey, a raccoon, and a coatimundi. She now
lives with her family in the foothills of the Blue Ridge Mountains, where she enjoys hiking,
painting, and snuggling with their cats Pocket, Pebble, and Mr. Tree-Tree Triggers.

CONTENTS

CHAPTER 1

The Story People Tell

Apples for All

Poems, rhymes, and children's books tell the story of Johnny Appleseed. He was born in Pennsylvania just before the start of the American Revolution (1775–1783). Johnny Appleseed wanted to feed the world, the story says. Pioneers and settlers were moving west. It was not easy to find food. Johnny wanted to help these pioneers. He wanted to make sure that none of them ever went hungry.

He took his leather bag and filled it with apple seeds. Then he picked up his Bible and his cooking pot. He wore the pot on his head for a hat. He did not wear shoes. The skin on his feet was so thick that he could walk on ice and snow. It was also so tough that not even a rattlesnake

People said Johnny Appleseed always carried a Bible and never wore shoes.

could bite through it. Johnny did not need much clothing, either. Instead of a shirt, he wore a coffee sack. He did not carry a knife or gun for protection. He was not worried about any danger on the frontier. He was kind to the wild animals. They were his only companions as he traveled.

Johnny was also kind to everyone he met. He handed ribbons to children he met. He read to them from his Bible in the evening. He refused beds and slept on the floor. He would not eat with families unless he was sure there was enough for the children.

The legend says that Johnny Appleseed spread apple seeds wherever he roamed. As a result, apple trees grew everywhere he'd been!

As Johnny walked, he looked for places to plant his apple seeds. Every time he found a good spot, he reached into his bag, grabbed some seeds, and scattered them. Soon the seeds began to grow. There were apple trees in open places in the forests. They grew along the roads and beside streams. They produced plenty of big, red, juicy apples to eat.

Because he planted so many apple trees, Johnny Appleseed didn't need to worry about settlers going hungry on their travels.

Johnny planted trees across the West, all the way to California. Along the way, he made a lot of friends. He was a gentle and humble man, and people were thankful for the apple trees. Soon there were so many apples that Johnny did not have to worry about the settlers being hungry. Johnny had spent his whole life planting apple seeds. He was only sick one day. That was the day he died.

Many statues of Johnny Appleseed can be found throughout the United States today, especially around the Appalachian Mountains.

The story of Johnny Appleseed is one of kindness and gentleness. It is a story about farming, too. It shows how important farmers are. It is also a story about living a simple life. Johnny Appleseed did not need fancy clothes. He did not need money. Finally, the story of Johnny Appleseed shows how small acts, such as planting a seed, can grow and make a big difference later.

Many of the details of Johnny Appleseed's story come from St. Francis of Assisi. St. Francis is a Catholic saint. He is famous for befriending animals. He traveled Europe in simple clothes. He followed the teachings of Jesus Christ. Johnny Appleseed's story shows Johnny as a holy man.

CELEBRATING A LEGEND

Every September, the city of Fort Wayne, Indiana, hosts the Johnny Appleseed Festival. The event celebrates the life of Johnny Appleseed. Johnny is buried somewhere along the St. Joseph River in Fort Wayne. No one knows the actual site. But a grave marker is in Johnny Appleseed Park. Each year during the festival, children place apples beside the marker.

Aside from statues, other art has been made depicting Johnny Appleseed, like this mural.

The real story of Johnny Appleseed is different. The real story isn't about feeding hungry people. Instead, the real story is about real estate, government policy, and religion. But it is also about a strange man in a coffee sack walking barefoot from place to place. The facts might just be more interesting than the fiction people have spun about him.

CHAPTER 2

The Facts of the Matter

A Frontier Businessman

Johnny Appleseed was a real person. His name was John Chapman. He was born in Leominster, Massachusetts, on September 26, 1774. His parents were Nathaniel and Elisabeth Chapman. He had an older sister and a baby brother. But when Chapman was less than 2 years old, his mother and brother became sick and died. At the time, Chapman's father was serving in the **Continental Army**. Chapman and his sister went to live with relatives.

After the war, Chapman's father returned, married again, and had 10 more children. Chapman grew into a slender young man of medium height. He had light brown hair and blue eyes. He became an **apprentice** to a farmer who had apple orchards.

Many claim this photograph to be of the "real Johnny Appleseed," or John Chapman.

The original Ohio Company land office still stands today in Marietta, Ohio.

In 1800, the U.S. government began selling land northwest of the Ohio River. The government was in debt. The American Revolution was expensive. The U.S. government claimed the land northwest of the Ohio River. A group of land **speculators** formed the Ohio Company. They bought 1.5 million acres (607,028 hectares). The land was already inhabited by Indigenous peoples. Among them were the Wyandot, Lenapi, Miami, Shawnee, Ojibwe, Odawa, Potawatomi, Cherokee, Creek, and others. Members of these groups formed a confederacy to defend their land. They fought the company representatives who tried to settle the land. So, the government decided to give the company another 100,000 acres (40,469 ha). This land would be a buffer between the American settlers and the Indigenous peoples.

The Ohio Company offered a deal to people who might want to settle in the buffer area. Any White male who built a permanent homestead would receive 100 acres (40 ha) of land. To prove they were going to stay,

ALONE, BUT NOT A LONER

Through the years, Chapman kept in touch with his family. They had moved to the Ohio territory in 1805. Although Chapman did not settle down with them, he visited them regularly. He remained close to them his whole life. In 1842, Chapman made his last trip back to Ohio to live with his **half brother** Nathaniel. Chapman never married and never had any children.

the settlers had to build a cabin, clear land for pasture, and plant 50 apple trees and 20 peach trees. John Chapman had an idea. He could plant the apple orchards and acquire the land. Then after a few years, he could sell the young trees or rent the land to new settlers.

At the time, apple orchards already existed in many places throughout the Ohio River Valley. French traders had brought apples to the region 200 years earlier. Indigenous women in the regions were responsible for farming. They planted crops to support the community and trade with others. They planted orchards and tended to the trees. The story of Johnny Appleseed ignored this.

When he was about 25, Chapman planted his first apple tree **nursery** in northern Pennsylvania. Then he moved into central and northwestern Ohio and eastern Indiana. He thought carefully about where settlers would go. He plotted routes he thought they would use. Then he traveled ahead of the settlers on those routes. First, he chose a planting spot. Next, he fenced it in with fallen trees and logs. Then he planted apple seeds he had collected from **cider mills**. He paid a neighbor to take care of the nursery and sell the trees. Then he moved on. Every couple of years, he returned to check on the trees and repair the fences.

Indigenous women were taking care of apple trees in the Ohio River valley before the legend of Johnny Appleseed.

Chapman continued to buy more land and planted the seeds farther west. Along the way, he picked up the name Johnny Appleseed.

Even though Chapman had plenty of money, he appeared to be very poor. He walked everywhere he went. He traveled barefoot, even in the winter. He wore the worst clothing people gave him. He gave everything else to someone who needed it more. At times, he was seen wearing a sack with holes cut in it for his arms and legs. He may have worn a tin pot on his head, a cardboard hat, or someone else's old hat. At night, he slept on the ground with his feet facing a small fire.

Chapman was part of a religious group called the Swedenborgian Church. This church followed the teachings of a man named Emanuel Swedenborg. The teachings said that the more a person suffered in life, the more that person would be rewarded in heaven after death. Chapman carried his Bible and Swedenborgian literature everywhere he went. He preached to the people he met on his travels.

Chapman cared deeply about animals. He was a vegetarian. He even refused to ride a horse. He thought it was cruel.

Chapman spent 50 years wandering as far west as Illinois. He planted nurseries and individual apple trees across 100,000 square miles (259,000 square kilometers) of midwestern farmland and prairie. Some evidence exists that he may have claimed Indigenous orchards as his own. By the end of his life, he owned 1,200 acres (486 ha) in Pennsylvania, Indiana, and Ohio. On March 18, 1845, Chapman became sick and died. He had been visiting a friend. He might have had **pneumonia**. He was 70 years old.

CHAPTER 3

Spinning the Story

A Model of Kindness

John Chapman's life was unusual, even for people 200 years ago. People talked about the strange man and shared stories about him. One of the first printed stories was an article by W. D. Haley in 1871. Haley supported an organization that helped farmers. He thought Chapman was the perfect example of what the organization stood for. Chapman was frugal, never spending any money on himself. He was also a religious man who helped others whenever he could.

An etching of John Chapman in an 1871 issue of *Harper's New Monthly Magazine*. This was the same year W. D. Haley's article on John Chapman appeared in the magazine.

Rosella Rice was well-known for her girlhood
accounts of John Chapman.

Haley published his article in *Harper's Monthly Magazine.* In it, he did not just describe John Chapman. He wrote about Johnny Appleseed. He talked about how Johnny walked barefoot into areas where black rattlesnakes lived. He told how Johnny was so good that the rudest frontiersman treated him with respect. Haley wrote that even the Native Americans battling settlers welcomed Johnny with kindness. Haley also wrote about the day Johnny died. He said that Johnny was glowing with heavenly light.

Others added to Johnny Appleseed's myth. One of these was a woman named Rosella Rice. John Chapman had visited her home in Ohio when she was a little girl. She wrote about her memories of him. Then she gathered more stories from others in the area. In the early 1880s, Rosella published some of these accounts in national magazines. She said that Johnny chose the most beautiful sites in the forests for his apple trees. She also claimed that nearly every orchard in the settlements came from Johnny's nurseries.

Another person who added to Johnny Appleseed's story was a writer named Lydia Maria Child. In 1881, she wrote a poem titled "Apple-Seed John." She wanted to show how anyone can do something to help someone else. The poem talks about poor Johnny who wanted to do something to

THE MYTH KEEPS GROWING

A 1948 Disney cartoon also helped shape the myth of Johnny Appleseed. It focuses on a person's ability to make a difference. In the story, Johnny feels like he's too small and weak to do anything important. Then a guardian angel convinces him all he needs is his faith, his Bible, and some apple seeds. Johnny sings a song that has become known as "Johnny Appleseed Grace." Some people think John Chapman wrote it, but it was actually

Lydia Maria Child wrote (in her poem "Apple-Seed John") that John Chapman received apples for pay when he helped others.

help others. He worked hard and received apples for pay. After cutting out the cores, he headed out and planted them. When he ran out of apples, he'd go back to the cities and earn some more. He was successful in his mission. People enjoyed the fruit long after he was gone. In the years after the poem was published, the story of Johnny Appleseed

CHAPTER 4

Writing History

Finding Evidence

Some people write in diaries or journals. Some write personal letters to friends and family members. All these documents help historians learn about people in the past. But very little was written about the real John Chapman. The earliest publication about him was a report by the Manchester Swedenborgian Society in England. It was written in 1817.

The report gives details about Chapman and his activities. It mentions how he traveled without shoes and could thaw ice with his bare feet. It tells how Chapman could live inside or outside with very little food. It also describes Chapman's apple tree nurseries. The report said they were each 2 to 3 acres (0.8 to 1.32 ha) in size. It also tells how Chapman worked as a missionary for his church. He used the money from the apple trees to buy books

Emanuel Swedenborg was the founder of the Swedenborgian Church.
John Chapman worked as a missionary for the church.

containing Emanuel Swedenborg's teachings. Then he would give the books to people he met. Sometimes he would divide a book into two or three parts. That way, he could share it with more people.

The earliest U.S. publication about John Chapman was his **obituary**. This account appeared in the *Fort Wayne Sentinel* newspaper in 1845. It describes John Chapman as a man with a large amount of property who lived on very little. It also mentions how he shared the teachings of his religion. The article also says that Chapman was well-known because of his strange clothing. One witness said that when Chapman died, he was wearing a rough coffee sack with a hole cut out for his head. Chapman's pants consisted of scraps of cloth buttoned together. But the scraps were not enough to protect him from the cold, and he died of the "winter plague."

HOME-GROWN APPLES

The Swedenborgian Church did not allow its members to **graft** apple trees because it hurt the trees. So Chapman planted seeds instead. But grafted trees produced tastier fruit. Because John's trees all grew from seeds, the apples were small and sour. They were not good to eat, but they were good for making cider and vinegar. Many adult settlers drank cider instead of water. At that time, water often had bacteria in it that made people sick. Settlers used the vinegar to pickle vegetables and store them for winter.

After Chapman died, people began publishing stories about him. The legend of Johnny Appleseed grew. About 100 years later, historians and **genealogists** began searching for the real John Chapman. They looked through old church books. These contain records of births, marriages, and deaths. They found information about Chapman and his family. They found his father listed in military records. Historians also searched store ledgers and land records to learn about Chapman's purchases. **Census** records helped them discover when Chapman and his family moved. Maps showed where he lived. Finally, they were able to put the pieces of Chapman's story together.

There is no doubt that John Chapman was an unusual character. He was a generous friend, a shrewd businessman, and a devout follower of his church. The myth of Johnny Appleseed grew because it was made to show Johnny Appleseed as an American folk hero, leading American settlers west. The story ignored the fact that the land was already inhabited. It ignored the fact that Indigenous peoples were already growing orchards. It ignored the aftermath of war and the battles the Indigenous confederacy waged to defend their land. Finding the true story helps us better understand history as well as how our world today came to be.

Activity
Be a Taste Tester

The apples that Johnny Chapman grew were sour. Do you like sour or sweet apples? Which kind is your favorite? If you don't know yet, you can be an apple taste tester!

Supplies:

Apples — at least five different varieties. Some common varieties found in a grocery store include Red Delicious, Golden Delicious, Granny Smith, Pink Lady, Gala, Honeycrisp, and Fuji.

Cutting knife

Paper plates — one for each type of apple

Pen or pencil

Paper

Blindfold

1. Find a parent or another adult to help.
2. With the adult's help, slice one of the apples.
3. Place the pieces of the apple on one of the paper plates.
4. Write the name of the apple on the plate.
5. Repeat for each variety of apple.
6. On the paper, write down the name of each apple. Leave some space under each name.
7. Circle the name of the apple you think you will like the best. Put a square around the one you think you will like the least.
8. Have the adult tie a blindfold around your eyes. Make sure you cannot peek.
9. Once your eyes are covered, have the adult hand you one of the plates.
10. Take a bite of the apple. Have the adult write your first impression under the name of the apple. Is it sour? Is it sweet? On a scale of 1 to 5, how much do you like it? Use "1" for "not at all" and "5" if it could be your favorite.
11. Repeat for each variety of apple.
12. When you have tasted each apple, remove the blindfold. Which apples did you like best? Which ones did you not like? Were your guesses correct?

Learn More

Books

Adil, Janeen. *Johnny Appleseed.* New York: NY: AV2, 2020.

Harasymiw, Mark. *Johnny Appleseed.* New York, NY: Gareth Stevens Publishing, 2018.

Smith, Andrea. *Johnny Appleseed.* New York, NY: PowerKids Press, 2012.

Talbot, Jeffrey. *Johnny Appleseed.* New York, NY: Cavendish Square, 2014.

On the Web

With an adult, explore more online with these suggested searches.

"Johnny Appleseed's Journey," PBS Learning Media

"Johnny Appleseed's Legacy Lives on in Fort Wayne," Fort Wayne, Indiana

"Johnny Appleseed Was Born," America's Library

"The Story of Johnny Appleseed," Washington Apples

Glossary

apprentice (uh-PREN-tuhs) someone learning a job through experience under a skilled worker

cider mills (SYE-duhr MILZ) places with the equipment for crushing apples into apple juice to make apple cider

census (SEHN-suhss) an official count of the people who live in an area, including information about their age and gender

Continental Army (kahn-tuh-NEHN-tuhl AHR-mee) the army representing the 13 colonies in the American Revolution

genealogists (jee-nee-AH-luh-jists) people who study records showing the ancestors of a person or group

graft (GRAHFT) a part of a plant that is taken off and placed into a slit on another plant so that the two parts will grow together

half brother (HAF BRUH-thuhr) a male who is a brother through one parent

nursery (NURH-suh-ree) a place where plants or trees are grown for sale

obituary (uh-BIH-chuh-wehr-ee) a printed announcement of a person's death

pneumonia (nuh-MOH-nyuh) a serious disease in which the lungs become swollen, painful, and filled with liquid

speculators (SPEH-kyuh-lay-tuhrz) people who purchase large amounts of land cheaply and sell it again for a higher price

Index